BY CHRISTINA M. LONG

B.global Publishing

Copyright © 2019 by CHRISTINA M. Long

All rights reserved.

Published in the United States of America by B. Global Publishing.

Photograph credits appear on page 100

ISBN 9780996589987

Printed in the United States of America

Book design by Christina M. Long, CML Collective, LLC

Cover design: CML Collective, LLC

Cover photograph by Tiffany N. Cody

Publication editor: Cathy I. Davis

No part of this publication may be used or reproduced in any manner — except for brief quotations in critical reviews or articles — without the written permission of the author.

Although every effort has been made to ensure the accuracy and completeness of the information contained in this book, the author, producer, publisher and printer disclaim any liability, either directly or indirectly, for any infringement of copyright, or otherwise, arising from the contents of this publication.

First Edition

Dedicated to:

My Husband, Jonathan, who showed me greater.

My children, Amarah, Malcolm and Jordyn, the hope of my heart and the gifts of my life.

My entire family ... for everything.

Kaci, who always knew. Rest well, Sister.

My Lord whose purpose magnified my life and amplified my faith.

And to each and every person who poured into me, together, we designed a decade in ways **that changed my entire life.**

"I need to take up space," ... *"I can do this. I am experienced enough to do this. I am knowledgeable enough to do this. I am prepared enough to do this. I am mature enough to do this. I am brave enough to do this."*

- Entertainment Weekly article quoting Rep. Alexandria Ocasio-Cortez "Meet the New Political Doc Stars, from Beto to AOC" April 15, 2019

I AM HERE.

700 people witnessed the moment when I realized I was "here."

April 26, 2018, I stepped to the podium at the Wichita Regional Chamber of Commerce's Honors Night to accept the second-ever Exceptional Young Leader Award. It was the same year that Ryan Coogler's *Black Panther* was released and culture was lit. Wakanda Forever. And, here I was. Standing before the city's elite; the corporate powerhouses and top philanthropists there to recognize some of the city's top leaders.

And I was among them.

I opened my mouth and spoke my heart in a six-minute monologue that wove listeners through my faith journey when the Lord put his hand on the mouth of Jeremiah and said, "I am watching over my word to perform it"; to the uneasiness I first felt being invited into boardrooms to sit at tables defined by white male privilege and power to those same men making room for me. I led them through the appreciation I felt for people who stood up for me — from helping me navigate rooms to those who styled me to ensure I "looked the part" — to my mentors and family members who, as I said, watched me go from having a byline to being a headline. I spoke about my husband, who allowed our home décor to be white boards and strategic plans. And I made an ask. I asked those in that room to find someone uncommon, find a point of commonality and do the extraordinary. When it was time to close my comments I summoned all who had come before and all who were to come. I said this was "our win", crossed my arms over my chest to

signal "Wakanda Forever" and I exited the stage to what would be one of the first standing ovations in the history of Honors Night.

People swarmed me through the dessert reception. They cheered me on for speaking about my faith. They admired my confidence, my vulnerability and my message. They vowed to connect with me… so we could do the extraordinary.

I took up space that night.

14 MONTHS LATER...

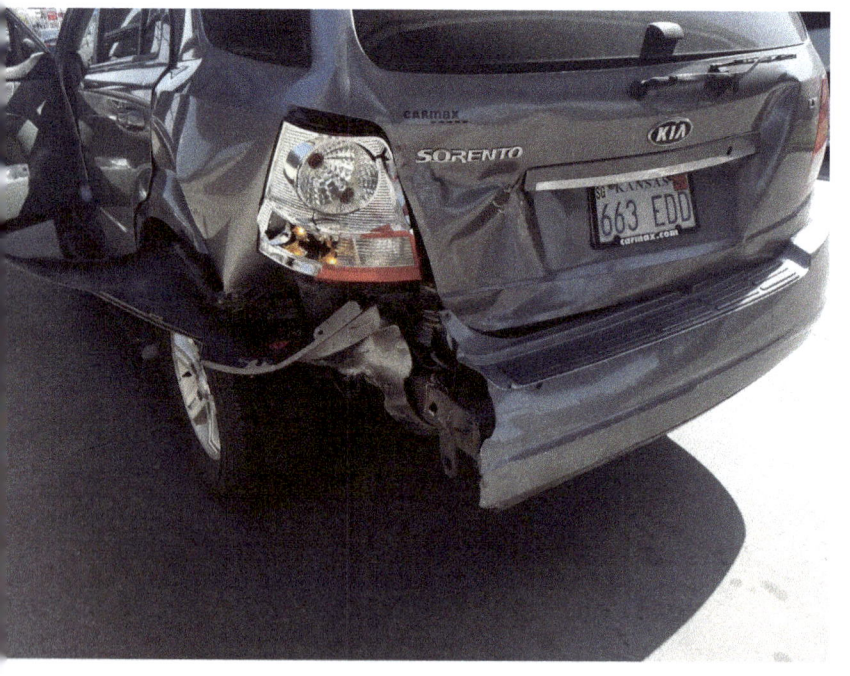

I sat in my bedroom exhausted, drained and on the verge of a nervous breakdown. A building had been gifted to my nonprofit and it needed renovations to become a hub for minority entrepreneurs who I served so diligently through my nonprofit organization, Create Campaign, Inc. I had more than $400,000 left to raise. My nonprofit was carrying the overhead for the building and we were hemorrhaging money.

My for-profit graphic design and communications company, CML Collective, LLC, was experiencing tremendous growth, but I lacked the staffing to help manage the growth and balls were dropping all over the place. Worst of all, my personal finances were overextended and an untimely totaling of my car from being rear-ended did my credit no favors.

I felt anything but exceptional when I came across Rep. Ocasio-Cortez's words.

Tears filled my eyes and I thought about the need to take up space — or as I've reinterpreted them: the need to magnify. I couldn't shake it. I took in her words over and over again.

"I can do this," she said.

Yes, I could raise the money needed to complete renovations at the building, I told myself.

"I am experienced enough to do this," she said.

I spent more than half of my life in newsrooms as a journalist. Six years of that time was spent telling stories of minority communities and people. After that, I would go on to lead a division in the largest school district of the state where my work involved creating curriculum for principals and teachers on ways to better engage communities and families to support student success. I launched an award-winning graphic design and communication services company; began serving on the board of directors with the Wichita Regional Chamber of Commerce and began connecting minority entrepreneurs with organizations that could help them start and grow their businesses through the Create Campaign. The nonprofit work led to the launching of a microloan fund driven by private dollars, which allowed our lending to be based on broader credit and collateral requirements, which meant we were able to loan business funds to minority business owners who would otherwise face rejections, most likely. We formalized our work in 2017 as a nonprofit and, one year later, our nonprofit was gifted a building which was an underperforming branch of a bank that my family used to bank at when I was younger. The bank sets fewer than 10 city blocks from the neighborhood I grew up in.

"I am knowledgeable enough to do this." I had been invited by a major foundation to help advise their grant making and criteria processes. A statewide nonprofit contracted with me to expand my minority business development work to the fourth-largest county in our state. Presentation requests about my efforts and successes spanned from high schools to the largest Rotary chapter in my city to the Federal Reserve Bank of Kansas City.

"I am prepared enough to do this." I managed to grow my nonprofit to serve more than 1,500 Black and Brown entrepreneurs in four years. A key handful of entrepreneurs worked our program so well, they not only launched, structured and branded their company but they were able to establish brick and mortar locations in the heart of downtown Wichita. One was even able to attract investment dollars.

This wasn't overnight success. I'd been working in the field of advancing minority populations — be it through journalism, education or entrepreneurship — for more than 15 years.

"I am mature enough to do this." Just in my 30s, I spent an entire decade working on self-improvement and uplift through a process I dubbed (and hashtagged) #designingmydecade. Rather than New Year's resolutions, I make birthday resolutions and, on the eve of my 30th birthday, I decided to forego that tradition replacing it, instead, with making a series of promises and commitments to myself to improve my life from good to great so that, when I turned 40, I'd be living the life I imagined. Author Stephen Covey, who wrote *7 Habits of Highly Effective People*, inspired my promise-making as one of his habits reads, "Begin with the End in Mind." I thought about what my life would look like if all of my commitments and promises came true and all I could imagine was the singer Janet Jackson's face on the cover of her album, "Design of a Decade."

She looked at peace. Happy. Free.

I committed to a better me and that process, alone, changed my life.

"I am brave enough to do this."

But I wasn't. Not at that moment.

I was risk-adverse; cautious; overwhelmed and feeling alone. Despite having an incredible personal and professional support system and people who helped me achieve all that I had accomplished thus far, I was scared out of my mind that I would make a mistake, a wrong move, and that the promise of what was to come through the building, my nonprofit, my company, and even my personal finances, would not see the level of success that I believed was necessary to underscore the progress and achievement I envisioned.

So, I cried.

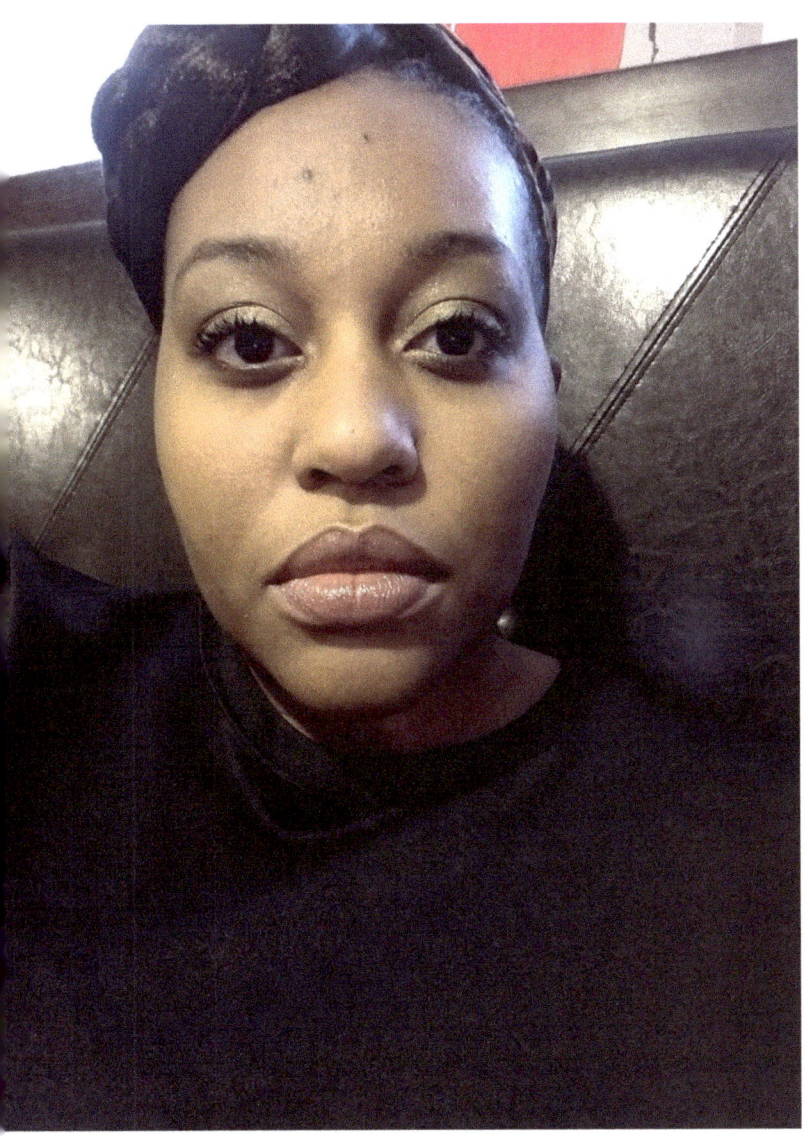

Then I stopped. With a renewed energy from absorbing her words, I raced to retrieve every notebook that I had. The pages in these books contained details of projects, brainstorms, plans and, most importantly, quotes. These quotes were moments of inspiration that I jotted down when meeting with my mentors, various leaders, clients and from hours upon hours of strategic planning with my husband.

These conversations held in coffee houses, and board rooms, offices and over the phone, have become near sacred to me. They're core to my ability to navigate spaces where I'm not supposed to be; to connect with people who are far beyond my circle of influence and pay grade. These notebooks and their content represent the journey traveled to become the influencer people say that I have become.

Alone, though, they tell half of my story. The other half is detailed in my journals; the books that have chronicled the life lessons borne from sorrow, misery, defeat and conflict. Through poetic prose or tear-streaked stream of consciousness passages, the words captured in in these texts also helped to, ultimately, **SET ME FREE!**

Together, the lessons from my notebooks and journals combine moments of awareness and awakening from incredible people. These writings have helped me to "take up space." They've helped me to create a path that is, authentically, mine and that, as imperfect as it may be, has inspired so many. And, even on the days, when I feel overwhelmed, underestimated or even unworthy, they remind me that, yes, I am here and that I've got work to do.

This book is for those who are at the intersection of inspiration and action. Those wanting to amplify life. Change agents. The visionary. Those who are young. The diverse. The savvy. Entrepreneurs. Corporate and community leaders. The driven.

It's for all of those who wish to impress upon the world that you, too, are here.

Now, let's claim our space.

part *one*

The *journey* to Me

be *Independent*
women of
independent means

My mother is a jewel.

She's one of the most complex and complicated people I've met. She's brilliant and stubborn and amazing.

Since we were young girls, my two younger sisters and I had the pleasure of having our mother tell us, "Be independent women of independent means."

She and my father did their best to make sure we were just that.

My Mom decided when we were toddlers that, if we could talk, we had the ability to read.

And she taught us.

By age three, I was reading *Green Eggs and Ham*.

Most nights, my Dad would tuck us in bed and recite "Goldilocks and the Three Bears" or St. John 1:1-13: "In the beginning was the Word, and the Word was with God and the Word was God..."

By kindergarten, I was tested for the "Gifted and Advanced" program.

We were surrounded with love, books and reminders that we had to work hard. We had to meet the standard. It didn't matter what anyone else was doing. We owed it to ourselves to do our best, be honest, don't cheat—ever — and to remember that character is doing the right thing even if no one is watching.

My parents taught us to double and triple check our work; that anything having our name on it should reflect our excellence. That we are not to take that which did not belong to us—including not cheating our employers of their time by goofing off at work or taking office supplies as our own. It meant putting our heads down and getting tough assignments completed and not complaining through the process. It meant doing what needed to be done and not waiting for anyone to tell us.

Today it's called being a "self-starter." Growing up, it was being "Independent Women of Independent Means."

The bar was set high.

But my parents also had the bar set high by their parents.

For my Dad, the high bar came when his parents told him that he wouldn't attend the all-Black junior high school that was just a few blocks from their home in central- northeast Wichita. Instead, my Dad became one of the first black students to attend Coleman Junior High School.

The bar was set.

For my Mom, the high bar was set by her mother who passed along a love of reading and learning that set her children on the path of success.

The bar was set.

My parents never wanted us to settle for mediocrity.

And, though it wasn't always easy, we didn't settle.

We figured out, in many ways, how to soar.

With the head start and the strong work ethic instilled, I knew I wanted to grow up and be a writer. I just didn't know what kind of writer I wanted to be. I soon found out in eighth grade. At the time, Joe Rodriguez and Mark McCormick were reporters at *The Wichita Eagle*. They visited my class and talked about being a journalist. I had no idea the career path existed before their visit. At the end of their talk, I remember they said that if anyone wanted a tour of the newsroom to contact them.

I did. I'll never forget walking through *The Wichita Eagle* that first time and meeting the press guys, hearing the whirl of the machine and smelling the fresh ink dry on the newsprint. The newsroom was even busier with reporters rushing past our group and the police scanner going off, blaring the latest happenings on the street. I knew I wanted to be there.

I kept in contact with Mark through the years. When I was a sophomore at East High, *The Wichita Eagle* was hiring positions for its "phone crew." Instead of going to my high school football games, I got to go to the newsroom and log scores from high school coaches calling them in from all over the state. It was thrilling being on "deadline" with the old sports guys listening to their banter in between phone calls. Mark also connected me with Bonita Gooch, the Publisher of the *Community Voice*, an African-American newspaper. I got a trial run with her writing a few stories where I was paid by the word.

I was getting real-world experience early.

And while my grades were good, I was one of four Black girls in East High's International Baccalaureate program (IB), an accelerated learning program. I eventually quit IB, though, after some racial incidences by parents prompted the only Black IB teacher at the time to leave the program. I followed her.

Still, journalism was my safe place. I ended up being named the editor of the school newspaper, the *East High Messenger*, had my *Community Voice* writing gig, I earned a few journalism scholarships for my writing and Mark even lined up several contacts for me at the University of Kansas, which resulted in me writing for the *Lawrence Journal-World* newspaper covering KU athletics. During that time in my life, he was an amazing mentor and coach.

I moved back to Wichita, though, after a series of losses in my family. I reconnected with *The Wichita Eagle* and earned my degree while working there in various staff positions. By the time I graduated college, they offered me a full-time reporting job.

Everything was lining up pretty well with my school and my soon-to-be career field.

My personal life following college was another matter.

By 24, I was the mother of my oldest two children by my ex; a man who came up through difficult circumstances and who was trying hard to make sense of his own life. The death of one of his closest friends, however, caused his life to spin out of control and I was left trying to figure it all out.

By 27, I'd had enough.

> *Have you ever looked at the person who you thought you "loved," but didn't recognize who was staring back at you?*
>
> *Have you ever been at the intersection where the fairytale ends and reality begins? Where the person you've tried to improve, the potential you've been waiting on to appear, the lies you told yourself to prolong your relationship, all came undone.*
>
> *That's not love. That's wishful thinking and wishful thinking in the name of "love" is nothing more than a delusion. I know. I spent six years being delusional.*
>
> *The hardest part about ending my delusion was accepting the fact that I let myself down. I knew better, but wouldn't do better. I wanted so badly to be "in love" that I prolonged a relationship that mocked it...*

- September 27, 2008 blog entry

It was in this space that I met Gordon, a psychologist, who was a holdover from the hippie days. With one label, he helped to put my mistakes into perspective and helped me move onto the path of healing.

He called me a perfectionist.

And I rebuked him.

"How can you even call me that when my life looks like it does?" I told him. "If I'm such a perfectionist, why am I here?"

Remember, I was in my mid-20s and was a walking contradiction. On the one hand, I was a quasi-successful and respected journalist reporting for the city's largest newspaper. On the other hand, I was a single mother trying to get my life back. Was I angry? Yes. But in no way was I a perfectionist.

How. Dare. He.

Gordon was unmoved by my denial.

He leaned forward, pointed a finger in my face and said with conviction: "Your problem is, you don't know how to deal with life when life doesn't look like *you* think it should; when things don't go how *you* think they should go.

"YOU HAVE TO FIGURE OUT HOW TO MOVE ON WHEN LIFE DOESN'T GO YOUR WAY."

Epiphany made real. My rage instantly cooled. I was left numb. He got me. There was nothing else he needed to say, nothing else, at that moment, I needed to hear.

I never saw him again.

To some, the simplicity of "life isn't fair" is enough. But, I never understood why. I thought I did most everything the *right* way. Yes, I slipped every now and then, but I believed that being a person of faith, never doing drugs, graduating from college, working in my chosen career field, having an overly-optimistic demeanor and being loyal to the end was the recipe for living happily and satisfied. How wrong was I because I felt neither happy nor satisfied until that truth hit me.

In journalism, you're expected to get everything right; to be perfect in your reporting. Your credibility is at stake with every written word. You're expected to be an objective observer; in some instances even a bystander. Every conversation you carry, every encounter you have is tempered by the fact that you are your byline. You represent the company at all times.

Self gets silenced.

After that conversation with Gordon, I remember a conviction coming over me so strongly that it literally changed my sight. Lowering myself into my car after his session, I vowed to quit beating myself up for where I was in life and to balance my optimism with realism.

I began to work on me. I let go of the guy and focused on changing my life. I even changed my career once declining readership prompted a series of layoffs and furloughs at the newspaper. I joined Wichita Public Schools' Family Engagement Office. There, in that space, was a completely different and nurturing environment. Rather than perfection, we were expected to be our individual best for the collective good of our work team. In areas where one person was weak, another person was strong. Our leader, Jackie Lugrand, was a fearless visionary.

There, Riccardo Harris and I sat nearly back-to-back in a small office exchanging encouragement for all that was to come through activating the gifts within us. Another coworker, Stephanie Cousin, happened to know my family before I was born and had watched me grow up. A prayer warrior, Cathy I. Davis, kept us covered. Joseph Bowen spoiled us with his incredible baked goods.

I could go on about each and every person I worked with — that's how incredible our team was.

Life was looking a little brighter at 1:10 a.m. on Dec. 16, 2010 as I wrote in my journal: "I am blessed. I am surrounded by love. I am resilient. I. AM. 30!!!"

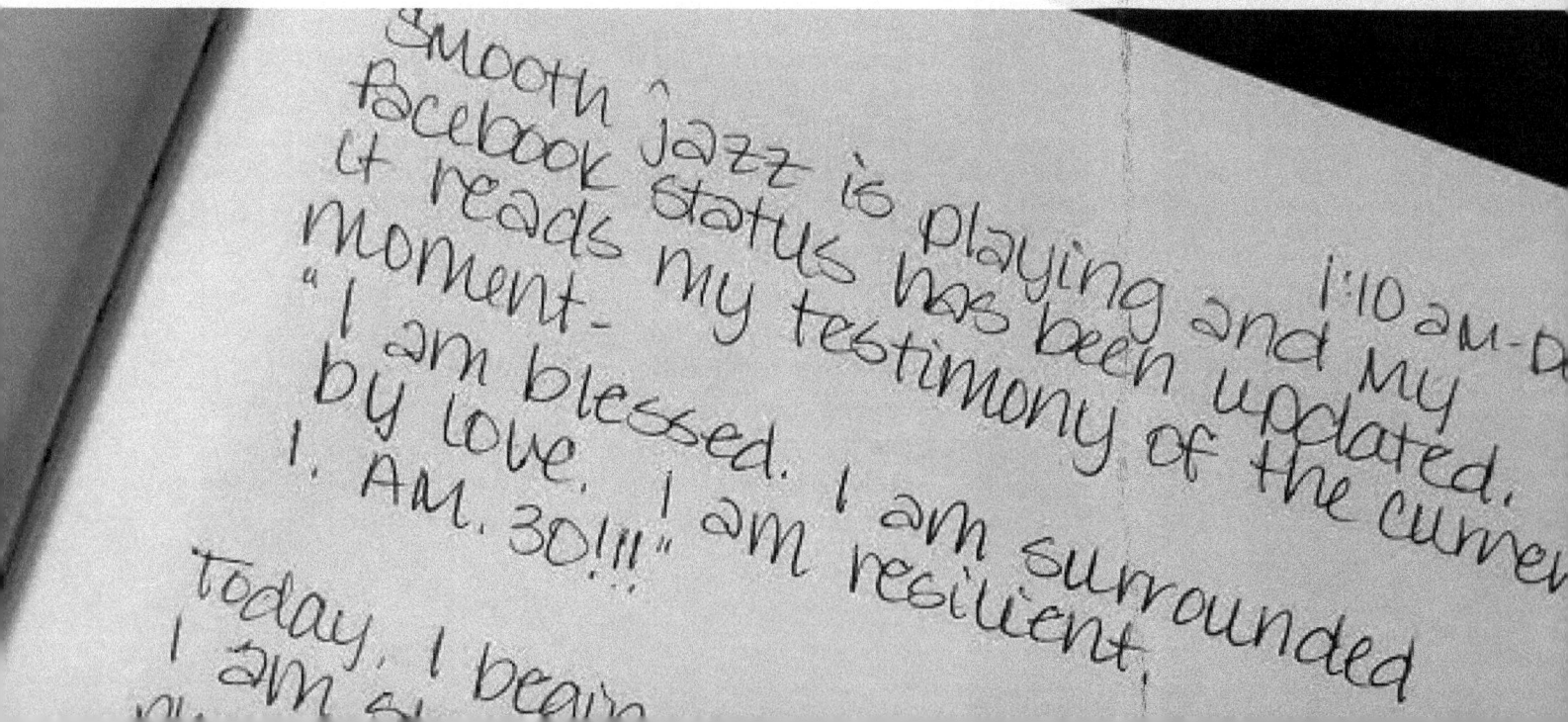

FOR THE greater SUCCESS

Take a moment and think about your path:

1. Who or what influenced you to become the person who you are today?

2. Describe one of the most defining teachings you received in your youth. How has that teaching influenced who you are present-day?

3. Describe a hurt from the past that you worked — or are continuing to work — to overcome.

4. What will it take to help you move beyond the hurt you previously described?

5. If you know what it will take to help you move beyond the hurt, why haven't you moved beyond the hurt?

Designing my decade

I don't make New Year's wishes. I make birthday wishes….

Ms. Jackie, my boss at the school district, had us read *The 7 Habits of Highly Successful People* by Stephen R. Covey, and when I read this habit: "begin with the end in mind" I thought: '*What do I want my life to look like when I turn 40?*'

Although I brought my best to each day, I was doing so outside of a real plan.

Could I bring my dreams to life?

After reading that book, a team member and I were talking and she casually said to me: "**THE DIFFERENCE BETWEEN A DREAM AND A GOAL IS A PLAN."**

Without actual steps, strategies and deadlines, our dreams and wishes will remain that – dreams and wishes.

I bought the best journal at Barnes and Noble and I promised myself that I had to act upon whatever I wrote in that journal. If it was good enough to be written in the journal, then it was good enough to work it into my life. No excuses. I was determined to design my decade.

I began to hold true to those promises. Throughout that time, I began discovering a new, stronger sense of self.

And I was loving it.

In that space, I met this guy who would eventually become my husband. Jonathan.

He thought he came from Tennessee to Kansas for a job. He really came for love.

My love.

He was everything I needed – in a package I didn't even know I wanted nor deserved. And facing what I thought was a dead-end on my search for love, he was my new beginning – the one who would lead me to a place I call "for keeps."

Through our love, I began to make better sense of me and the broken road I traveled before him. He came after my regrets, my hurts and my shame. He came as I was building a better me through an even deeper relationship with the One who created me. He came when I was most vulnerable and skeptical.

He came because God told him to come.

And he stayed because, as he says, he was "born to love me."

You don't play with a love like ours – a love that has healed and released the hurt from those who came before who mocked love's very existence.

No – in this place, for keeps means forever, for life everlasting and into the beyond. It's guaranteed. Not a fleeting hope, a whim or a wish.

It's that, "love you in a place, where there's no space or time."

It's that, "you gave me the kiss of life."

It's that, "I'll give you the breath that I breathe."

The forever, for always kind of love is what we found in each other. And now that love is leading us into a covenant before our Lord as signified by his question, cemented by my answer and symbolized in a beautiful ring once again proving that this love, his love is "for keeps."

- February 28, 2011 journal entry

When our fearless leader at work, Ms. Jackie, decided to retire, the remaining members of the team who were interested in her job had to interview for the position. There were people who had been with the District decades longer than I had and who had been doing the work for as long. When it came time to apply, my focus wasn't on them. It was on me. Interestingly enough, I felt an overwhelming sense of peace. Rather than worry about whether or not I was qualified for the job, I had a great sense of anticipation to showcase that I was *meant* for the job.

I nailed every question in the interview. I also had a portfolio as visual evidence of my knowledge and aptitude for the position. Usually, it's best practice to have a question to pose when you're asked, "Do you have any questions for us?" by the interview team. I told them I didn't, but that I'd like to use my time to walk through my portfolio with them and answer any questions they may have of me. Anyone who truly knows me knows I'm a humble person. Even in that moment, my enthusiasm was not perceived as arrogant. I was truly passionate about the position.

About an hour later, the phone rang and I was offered the job.

Throughout the entire interview process, this quote I wrote down in my journal came to mind:

"SUCCESS HAPPENS WHEN PREPARATION MEETS OPPORTUNITY."

I prepared. I had the opportunity and I landed the position, which I held for three years before I made another life-changing transition.

I launched my own company.

Here are a few recommendations I'll share to encourage you to design your own decade:

1. In 10 years, will you have the life you want to live if you keep living exactly as you're currently living?

2. If the answer is no, what do you want your life to look like 10 years from now? Be specific and look at your life in various areas such as faith, finances, family, fitness, etc.

3. To create the life you'd like to live, what must you do RIGHT NOW to initiate these changes?

4. Complete this sentence: I am worthy of _____ _____ because I am _____ _____.

part *two*

The *journey* to Greater

A magazine article changed the course of my professional career.

Rather than a newsletter, we launched a magazine called *Urbane Magnate* through my husband's organization, Wichita Urban Professionals. I was the founding editor. One of the stories I ended up covering was all of the momentum in our city around entrepreneurship and technology. I felt like there was so much happening downtown and at Wichita State University that, if communities of color didn't plug in, we'd miss out.

My research led me to interview Gary Oborny of Occidental Management. In our first conversation, we talked about what was happening with the Entrepreneurship Task Force (ETF), which was affiliated with the Wichita Regional Chamber of Commerce at the time. The ETF was working to accelerate economic development through entrepreneurship in the city. Wichita, after all, is the birthplace of great companies: Pizza Hut, White Castle, Freddy's Frozen Custard & Steakburgers, Koch Industries, Rent-a-Center and, even incredible products such as Mentholatum, to name a few.

What stood out in my first conversation with Gary was our discussion on the concept of why there wasn't a lot of growth in Black-owned businesses in Wichita. I explained some of our plight: Historic and systemic barriers, downright discrimination – think Black Wall Street, lack of capital, lacking credit, subjectivity in loan practices and the idea that most of us are trained to go to school, get a good job and be a good employee; not to open our own companies. We don't celebrate entrepreneurs like we should in our community. Entrepreneurship is just not really talked about. Additionally, with all of the odds stacked against African-Americans, the tolerance for risktaking is low.

There can be no failure.

To Gary, however, entrepreneurship is all about taking risks. It's also about failing. Gary explained failure as a learning tool.

"WHEN YOU FAIL, YOU FAIL FAST AND GET BACK UP AND DO IT BETTER," he said.

I was shocked when he said that. Then, I was angry – not with him— but with circumstances which allow certain groups to experience the ***privilege of failing.***

By the end of the conversation, Gary invited me to the ETF to be a co-leader of the African-American committee as it was called at that time.

I had no real background in entrepreneurship other than making a promise to myself to launch an outlet for positive messaging about women and people of color, as part of Designing my Decade. That promise led to me launching MSlady—a T-shirt company — while I was still working at the school district.

Despite my hesitation, I accepted Gary's invitation to attend an ETF meeting rather than just dismissing the idea outright.

What began as me testing the waters out at the ETF grew into me being a leader within the ETF. It took some time and I had to work through some things to gain confidence but I ended up leading the African-American committee and conceptualizing a new framework to support business development growth among minority entrepreneurs, and specifically African-Americans. I called the framework the Create Campaign.

Through my networks and my approach to community uplift, I was able to draw sizable crowds to Create Campaign events and many in the crowds followed up with area service providers who help develop and support business launches and growth. The Create Campaign helped these providers experience a shift in who their agencies were serving. The best part: I was able to create an environment where we could have challenging race/culture conversations to bring forth stronger awareness and understanding about how to serve minorities with cultural proficiency in mind.

I used to be the only African-American in the room. I used to be one of the youngest women making business presentations to longtime and well-known businessmen.

I didn't always feel equipped and, yet, doors opened in ways I couldn't even believe.

Back at the school district, as we entered the 2015-2016 school year, I remember thinking that it would be my last year with the district. My company was taking off and Create Campaign work was ramping up, as well. I wanted to focus on these efforts full-time. It was easily routine, during those times, to work my day job while using my lunch breaks, evenings, nights and weekends to work my company.

It was time for a change.

I boldly declared that March 4 was going to be my leave date. Why'd I pick that date? Not only was it symbolic — March *forth* —but, if I submitted my two-week notice on March 4, then the second of my two weeks would be Spring Break and I wouldn't have to work. It would give me a week to rest and transition to my new full-time work.

In December 2015, I was starting to get a little nervous. I didn't see how the jump was going to happen in March. After all, it meant leaving the security of my job to go full-time with my company.

In February 2016, one of the partners I worked with on the Create Campaign connected with me, shared how much they loved the work I was doing, offered to help me take it statewide and, in doing so, offered me a contract but, get this, through *my company*. The same day as my contract signing with that partner, another Create Campaign partner offered me part-time work hours to perform business development as an advisor with their center.

I ended that day in February that I now call my "signing day" with two opportunities that made up even more than 75 percent of my income that I was making with the school district. I was able to submit my two-week notice from my school district job on March 4.

You can't tell me God's hand was not at play!

FOR THE *greater* SUCCESS

Here are a few questions you may wish to reflect upon as you prepare for your greater:

1. Name a recent failure that you've experienced and the lesson you gained from that failure.

2. What is the change you're purposed to make? If you're unsure, dig deep. Think about a problem in your life, community or workplace that you're passionate about and what drives that passion.

3. Journal about what talent, gifts or characteristics you have that could help make the change in the area you're purposed to change or that you are passionate about.

4. Describe where you draw, or will draw, your confidence to move deeper into the work to make greater impact.

be the *Change*

Each and every one of us can influence the change we seek. More than just empty rhetoric, camera and photo ops, podcast episodes and social media posts, how we behave in moments of comfort and moments of strife signal whether or not change will be made.

Hope and wish all we want. Change doesn't occur until it meets an action.

When I think about true examples of those who were the change, I think back to the Civil Rights Movement of the 1950s and 1960s. There is brilliance within the Civil Rights Movement. I draw so much inspiration from the strength, conviction, discipline, determination and sheer bravery that men and women displayed for the sake of freedom and equality.

The Montgomery Bus Boycott, for example, is a wonder; particularly viewing it with today's filter where "fearing for our lives" has been repeatedly deemed as a credible defense absolving those who are targeting and assassinating Black bodies. While there are pockets of resistance — people and organizations doing incredibly difficult work — it never fails: slow-boiling anger bubbles over to feverish protests, the news cameras roll and social media erupts. Broadcast news fills cycles with talking heads who, though the names change, their positions remain the same – the agitator, the expert, the liberator and the moderator.

What, then, when all of the noise fades? What, other than sadness and outrage, is left?

Where's the change?

The Montgomery Bus Boycott was a case study in organization and what community sacrifice for community gain looks like. What other way to describe the systemic dismantling of discriminatory ridership policies is there? Imagine the sacrifice of walking, the level of coordination to move people in a manner outside of the norm to fight the discrimination of a people who were treated like anything but normal? The systemic dismantling required people to think beyond themselves; to offer rides to those who may have very well "gotten weak in well-doing" as the saying goes.

381 days of changed behavior through nonviolent mass demonstrations led to policy changes driven by people who were willing to be the change.

Let's bring it closer to my hometown.

Wichita, Kansas. The summer of 1958. Members of the Youth branch of the Wichita NAACP took to the lunch counters at the Dockum Drug Store to protest policies against discrimination in service. These youths, under the leadership of the late Ron Walters, had practiced in the basement of a church to prepare for their time at the counters. Their protest lasted just over three weeks and resulted in the successful desegregation of lunch counters at Dockum Drug stores in Wichita as well as the entire Rexall Drug Store chain across the state of Kansas.

Their victory inspired a similar sit-in to occur in Oklahoma City all prior to the now famous Greensboro sit-in that garnered national coverage and, though significant to the movement, eclipsed Wichita's. Not wanting to upset newspaper advertisers, the Dockum sit-in generated little local press coverage. The adult chapter of the Wichita NAACP didn't endorse the sit-in at the time because they felt it better to take action against discrimination in the courtrooms.

I had the great privilege of helping to tell the story of Dockum during my time at *The Wichita Eagle*. My reporting, along with the coverage of others such as Carla Eckels, helped the sit-in and the demonstrators gain proper recognition across the country – including by the National NAACP [See: "Updating History: NAACP agrees Wichita's 1958 Sit-In was First of Many" *The Wichita Eagle*, June 2, 2006 and "Wichita's Sit-In May Have Been First: NAACP plans to recognize 1958 lunch-counter act at its convention," *The Wichita Eagle,* June 8, 2006).

Their actions helped spur so many others in the name of equality.

When you take a look at the people who made great changes in the Civil Rights Movement and, truly, any other movement of significance in this nation, we tend to distinguish them from ourselves. We admire their stock, their determination, fearlessness and their grade when, in reality, many of us possess the same make-up.

Just like us, they stood on the shoulders of those who came before them like we stand on the shoulders of those who come before us.

We owe our past. We owe our future.

We owe our leadership.

We can be the change.

TO BE THE CHANGE,
HAVE CLARITY AROUND THE ISSUE YOU CARE MOST ABOUT

To understand how to be the change, you have to understand that **we are the ones we've been waiting for**. To influence change, you have to get in the game. Here are a few examples of ways to activate your leadership to be the change:

1. Have clarity around the issue you care most about – While you can make great impact across a multitude of issues, I firmly believe you can make deeper, more lasting impact by focusing your efforts and energies within one clearly-defined space. Why one? Think about it. When your mind is busy trying to multitask, you're only able to give each task a limited amount of attention and even that attention is distracted at best. On the other hand, when your mind is uncluttered and there is a clarity of focus, you bring your better self, more developed and dedicated thoughts and energy to that one issue.

I already sense the pushback: *with so many things in our communities that need fixing, how can I possibly focus on one issue? Wouldn't that make me guilty of operating in the same silo I argue against?*

I get it. I, too, thought if I was present in a number of areas, I'd gain community buy-in, backing and support for the efforts I really, truly cared about. I wore myself out and grew frustrated that my true area of interest— inclusive entrepreneurship — wasn't seeing the transformative progress I imagined it would.

But how could it? I was only dedicating a fraction of my energy and my time to this issue.

So I stopped being everywhere and got hyper-focused on inclusive entrepreneurship. No longer was I sitting at tables wearing multiple hats from different spheres of concern. I was clearly there to advocate and advance the work of creating more inclusive entrepreneurship practices and initiatives.

In doing so, my personal and professional brand was clarified. That clarity of purpose and brand helped to advance the work more effectively than I could realize prior to making the decision to be intentionally focused.

Before long, the same people who were initially critical about me serving in one area of community uplift became the same people who celebrated the advancements my nonprofit work was able to accomplish. I began to receive more requests within my sphere of interest and influence and was, not as often, pulled in multiple and disconnected directions.

One area. Focused impact.

TO BE THE CHANGE, UNDERSTAND WHO YOU ARE

"And why isn't being who you are as a child of God good enough for you… if it's good enough for God?" Iyanla Vanzant, *In the Meantime*

I stood in the doorway of the Wichita State University Hughes Metropolitan Complex clinging to my cell phone as my mentor, Dell Gines, put the challenge before me to step up. It was another one of our monthly mentoring phone calls in my early days of minority business development work through the Create Campaign. I was lost. And scared.

I was having an increasing number of people seeking my guidance on how to set up their businesses, get funding and grow. I felt unqualified to assist. True, I had launched a T-shirt company in 2013 while working a full-time job with Wichita Public Schools, as I previously mentioned. Before my company's second anniversary, so many people were asking me to design logos, flyers and even design websites, that I changed my company's name to CML Collective, LLC, expanded capabilities and became a full-scale graphic design and communications services firm starting in 2014.

When I say I was leading the ETF's African-American committee as a new entrepreneur, myself, I meant it. I only had two formal years of business under my belt when I held the first Create Campaign forum at Wichita State University to connect minority entrepreneurs to service partners whose work centered on helping businesses to launch and grow. That forum doubled the number of participants the Entrepreneurship Task Force planning team I was leading had hoped to attract to the event. Rather than 35 entrepreneurs, we had 77 African-American entrepreneurs who attended. It was so successful with people making connections, getting access to attorneys, banking contacts and small business development providers that I began to be sought out for business launching and growth advice that I felt unqualified to share.

Not only did I feel that I lacked the knowledge to expertly guide people along a more streamlined path to success, I felt like I was stepping into other organizations' lanes.

I didn't want to compete.

We had two emerging African-American Chamber of Commerces at the time. Our city's regional chamber didn't have a specific diversity and inclusion outreach component and the sentiment in the overall entrepreneurship community was that tech firms were more worthy of resources and development attention — not small, service-based companies, solopreneurs and the microenterprises that made up the Create Campaign Forum participants.

Dell, who serves as a community development advisor with a federal organization, was trying to impress upon me in that conversation that, if I was being sought out to provide information to people who were seeking help, not only should I provide information and be a resource, but I should do so with authority until other organizations could or would. For the time, I was the one positioned to be a resource so I should be that resource.

I definitely was battling with my comfort zone.

During that same time, I learned at a training at the Kansas Leadership Center that: **THE COMFORT ZONE IS A BEAUTIFUL PLACE. BUT NOTHING EVER GROWS THERE.**

It was time for me to grow, which meant I had to lean into my discomfort and do what was natural to me: be a connector and a communicator. I didn't have to be an expert, Dell said. I just needed to help connect people to information and communicate about resources along the way.

Dell was articulating what I now believe is critical of leadership: acting to make a change in manners authentic to us is a sound demonstration of leadership.

Rather than focusing on what information I lacked, I focused on how I could use what gifts were inherent within me — that had been nurtured and cultivated throughout the course of my entire life — to help make progress in the area of entrepreneurship and business development.

My thoughts changed from what I lacked to what I *could* do.

Although I had great interest and passion to help grow a stronger business base in the Black community, I also really felt that my role in the space was temporary; that another more established, better-resourced organization would step in and relieve me of my newfound responsibilities. Sure, I could coordinate an event to bring entrepreneurs and partners together. That was, in my mind, as "simple" as executing a strong event plan.

Never did I imagine that the work *outside* of the events —making connections, giving people advice and guidance — would be where I'd become more than a temporary fill-in.

If you find yourself at the critical juncture of change, it's imperative to understand who you are and understand what you're made of because insecurities will, otherwise, run rampant. If you're focused on your insecurities, you won't focus on the change you're positioned or *purposed* to make.

You — like I came to understand — are uniquely qualified to lead, to make progress, to be the change. And, if you've been positioned or purposed to do so, then you must. I say positioned because, unless you're already aware of the impact your change can have upon the problem or how executing on challenges impacts your purpose, then you being positioned to make a change is quite powerful.

Never overlook or undervalue the power of position. Your position places you in proximity to the challenge you're trying to improve and around people who you may not, otherwise, have an opportunity to interact with. Those people may open up resources you may not, otherwise, be privy to. Positioning can help to clarify the cause and your role within it.

In these instances, be mindful enough to recall Iyanla's words and ask, as I did: **WHO DO YOU THINK YOU ARE NOT?**

The answers may bring you to a different conclusion; a conclusion well beyond your fear.

In case you're still unclear about your position, then rest assured in the confidence of your faith knowing that **GOD DOESN'T CALL THE QUALIFIED. HE QUALIFIES WHO HE CALLS.**

FOR THE greater SUCCESS

Here are a few resources to help you discover more about yourself:

Take a personality test — I took my first personality test while working for Wichita Public Schools. Ms. Jackie believed in creating the best team by understanding our work styles, motivations and agitators. We took professional personality tests such as the Predictive Index, https://www.predictiveindex.com/.

Being able to understand key components about how you function, thrive and excel is essential.

Attend leadership trainings — I am a Kansas Leadership Center champion. The KLC, as those fond of the institution call it, creates intangible learning experiences centering on its interpretation of leadership as an activity; not a position. **"Anyone can lead, anytime and anywhere,"** a KLC principle states.

Through leadership training, we're equipped to understand how to dissect challenges and how to activate the leader within when exploring challenges. The courses are heavy, but well worth the time and financial investment. The institution has several books including *Your Leadership Edge*, which presents KLC's principles and core competencies in a rapid-read format.

Through KLC, I learned the vocabulary of leadership that helped me to better frame problems and better articulate potential solutions to everyday and complex challenges in life. Learn more about the Kansas Leadership Center by visiting: www.kansasleadershipcenter.org

Go to counseling – I've been blessed. My father, Minister Michael Woods, has always been a steady source of impartial and objective advice through my life. He has spent decades counseling on a number of fronts within our church and as my Dad. He's great at separating our relationship as "Father and Daughter" from being that of a counselor, which has been helpful.

Besides my Dad, there was Gordon who labeled me a "perfectionist." Both provided beneficial support in times of need.

The point is: there is no shame in seeking counsel from your support systems or professionals. Seeking counsel can help you reframe issues, speak from the heart and consider different ways to approach personal or life challenges.

Equipping ourselves to make great changes is quite taxing and having the strength to seek mental and emotional support and guidance can help fortify us for the work ahead.

FOR THE *greater* SUCCESS

Identify a release — and protect it – Music has always been a release for me. I'm the type of person who'll gladly turn off the television, put on some headphones or just crank my speakers up and let songs transport me from my current reality.

During a particularly hectic stretch of months, I knew life was out of sync when I stopped playing music. I didn't initially realize I quit playing music because I was too busy with heavy workloads to even realize the music in my home and office stopped flowing. In the car, zipping to and from meetings, I wouldn't even play music because I needed the silence to escape from all of the noise drowning my life.

It wasn't until I paused that I recognized I'd lost myself in work and I'd stop playing music.

To be in sync with oneself means to recognize when habits of comfort have been displaced because of the noise and busyness in our lives.

Whatever is your music, keep it flowing in your life. Protect that thing because it's your peace and your balance.

TO BE THE CHANGE KNOW THAT,
HATERS GON' HATE. DO WORK ANYWAY.

"Can't say nothing if you're last in the line. So when you diss, it just lets me know I'm on your mind, and it's all right." – Kris Kross, "Alright"

Having launched my company and working with the Create Campaign, I began to experience a series of sustained wins in my life starting in 2015. To name just a few:

- 40 Under 40 Class of 2015
- The Silver Royal Winner, Wichita American Marketing Association, Nonprofit Marketing (2016)
- Wichita Urban Professional Woman of the Year (2016)
- Leaders in Diversity, Wichita Business Journal (2018)
- The Minority Business Advocate of the Year by the Kansas Department of Commerce's Office of Minority and Women Business Development; my first statewide recognition (2018)
- At the time of this book's writing, I was notified that I earned a Women Who Lead in Professional Service recognition by the Wichita Business Journal (2019)

I used to shy away from these recognitions because, for me, it was never about the honors. It's always about the work.

However, I soon realized that, to access larger networks, people care about who you are and what you've accomplished. These types of recognitions help to provide distinction. They, too, are a necessary part in growing your influence and imprint.

Understand, though, that with much attention comes much more room for professional scrutiny—people questioning your motives, efforts and even the particulars of your impact.

When I was growing up, I always used to say: "If they dislike me, let me have earned that. Don't just dislike me for no reason."

Then, I began receiving recognitions for my accomplishments and the haters hated. Even people within my own community — those I assumed would be supportive because of our relationship, connections or simply on the strength of the fact that I was working to improve underestimated communities of color — were among the critics.

About the building that was gifted to my nonprofit: "Why did *she* get that building?"

Of the Create Campaign's work: "She doesn't even help people start companies." Never mind the fact that a partnership I formulated with one of the largest law firms in my state was knocking thousands of dollars off its pricing to perform business structuring and filing work. These filings were creating legally-recognized minority-owned companies in our state.

"She just helps people in her clique" … Then my clique is pretty big because my nonprofit's work has literally engaged hundreds in Kansas.

These were just some of the things people would say about me and my work.

There were times when I reduced my presence and tried to lessen the impact of my work to make room for others to feel even better about theirs. Seldom, did I respond publicly to negativity. And when I did, my response was the talk of social media.

I felt like, I could take the criticism but, at some point, people weren't going to just have a free reign on my name and my work. Some things needed to be spoken on and so I spoke.

Even then, no matter what I said or did; no matter what we accomplished through the nonprofit or, even what other people said on my behalf based on their *positive* experiences with me and my work, those who wanted to cause trouble, strife and dissension were intent to continue doing so.

Seeing this, I no longer gave time, space or attention to acknowledging their hate or pausing long enough to even concern myself with their opinions.

As Dell Gines shared with me about haters: **"THEIR LENS IS NOT BUILT FOR YOU, ANYWAY."**

My Mom puts it like this: **"YOU CANNOT FIX MISERABLE PEOPLE. THEIR ANGER IS NOT ABOUT YOU."**

"FIGURE OUT WHAT THE HIGH GROUND LOOKS LIKE AND HOW TO NAVIGATE IT," she says. **"PEOPLE WILL REJOICE IN YOUR DOWNFALL. DON'T GIVE THEM THAT VICTORY. GOD WOULD BE DISAPPOINTED IF YOU DID. HE'S BLESSED YOU WITH SO MUCH."**

Haters gon' hate.

Do your work anyway.

As my colleague Darrius Wright said during one of our coaching sessions: **"IF YOU'VE BEEN CALLED TO DO MEANINGFUL WORK, THEN YOUR WORK IS NOT TO MANAGE PERCEPTIONS; IT'S TO MAKE SIGNIFICANT IMPACT."**

After all, Darrius said, **"YOUR SUCCESS IS THEIR GREATER SUCCESS."**

Here are a few recommendations I have for avoiding the haters:

1. Mute distractions – Social media can be a tool for your benefit or your destruction. Know the difference between those providing constructive criticism and those who are bent on causing division and strife in your work and in your life. Silence those detractors and do so *guilt-free*. Everyone does not have to like you or your work. You cannot let everyone get the best of you by continuing to consume negativity.

2. Stop engaging in destructive conversations – Keep your ill feelings about people to yourself or to a very limited few. Conversing to others about those who have wronged you only keeps you stirring up the negativity you claim to want to distance yourself from.

Likewise, be mindful of how much negative information you allow to be brought to you.

FOR THE greater SUCCESS

3. Quit trying to impress people who do not like you or your work – Sometimes we go out of our way to try to validate our work to get detractors to see its worth. In short, this too, is an unnecessary exercise in impressing people who aren't worth our energy or time to impress. When we devalue our work and self by going out of our way to impress others who aren't meant for us — or the work — then we're being inefficient with our time and resources. The work is too important and our energy is too valuable to misspend.

4. Make a commitment to the work; not to being liked – As important as our work is, our work does not define who we are as people. When we take up a heavy or controversial task, we're putting ourselves in the line of someone else's opinion. We cannot be shaken or rattled from our work because of someone's opinion about us or our work.

As I always say, it's not about ego or being liked. It's about the impact we're trying to make. When we operate outside of the need to be comforted by others' approval, we're operating in freedom.

There's a book by Don Miguel Ruiz called The *Four Agreements*, where he shares four of his beliefs that, when put into practice, can help people live a drama-free life.

The belief that aligns closest with haters is: "Don't take anything personally."

He writes:

"...When we take something personally, we make the assumption that they know what is in our world, and we try to impose our world on their world."

He goes on to say: *"You are never responsible for the actions of others; you are only responsible for you. When you truly understand this, and refuse to take things personally, you can hardly be hurt by the careless comments or actions of others."*

Bottom line: Opinions can become some of the most powerful weapons against purpose-driven work. Don't let them.

Protect your spirit. Guard your peace.

TO BE THE CHANGE, DON'T THINK TOO SMALL

Sometimes life will show you that your viewpoint is a bit limited.

I remember sharing with several business leaders my thoughts on how to grow the Create Campaign and more times than not, they'd respond, "That's great, Christina, but don't think too small. Don't limit your viewpoint."

I didn't think my viewpoint was limited. I felt it was practical; so practical, in fact, I felt like I could obtain it with the limited resources I had.

It's interesting how viewpoints can impact our measure of achievement.

When we launched Wichita Urban Professionals' magazine, *Urban Magnate*, my husband was able to secure a downtown rooftop Penthouse for our release party. Standing outside as evening transitioned to nighttime with the city's twinkling skyline as a backdrop, I remember a woman standing beside me marveling at the view saying, "It looks so different from up here."

That night, it felt like we could take on the city. It looked like we were on top of the world and the possibilities were endless.

When the event concluded, I might have traveled down the elevator back to ground-level but the feeling never escaped me. The sense that Wichita can really look and feel HOW YOU MAKE IT look and feel was all over me.

This is the same type of feeling that materializes when you have access and when that access meets opportunity. It changes your view.

Dell Gines

At the critical junction when you're driving a vision, it's imperative that you **TRUST YOUR INSTINCT OVER YOUR FEARS**, Dell Gines, always says.

Don't give life to a limited perspective.

Instead, reframe your focus.

Rather than dwelling on what you lack, envision what you can do, who you can engage and what resources you can have if you had no barriers, no shortcomings, no shortfalls.

Imagine what success looks like on your issue, articulate that success and drive your focus towards that impact point.

Here are some prompts that may help you reframe your focus:

1. Write it down and make it plain: what challenge are you trying to address? What problem are you trying to solve?
2. What solution have you identified to help address the problem or the challenge?
3. What resources will you need to help you implement your solution?
4. Who can help you obtain those resources? What would be their motivation to assist you?
5. What is your ask of these people who can help you to obtain resources?
6. How will you know that you're making progress on addressing your challenge?
7. What does success look like when your problem or challenge is properly addressed by your solution?

who knows *You?*

Curtis Whitten is one smooth brother.

Neither his speech nor stroll are rushed. His smile is easy. His demeanor is chill. And when it comes to business, his acumen is prolific.

I attended church with Curtis and, during my childhood, my family visited his Black-owned bookstore that sat along a busy thoroughfare in Wichita, sandwiched amongst several fast-food restaurants in a strip mall. Entering the doorway of the bookstore, visitors would be greeted with his genuine handshake and covers from a number of genres of bestselling Black-authored books. I loved the store's displays because the book covers faced you as you scanned through the wooden bookshelves.

The visuals were powerful; the colors so warm and inviting. These titles weren't crammed in one section underneath an "African American" sign. No, these were our books and they spanned an entire store.

Although the store only lasted a few years, Curtis experienced great success launching a vending machine company followed by a security firm that thrived upon securing government contracts.

The company's contracts ranged from securing everything from people to airports. His revenue soared to the millions. He conducted his business expertly and became a quiet mogul in our city.

And, still, whenever I called upon him for advice, he made time for me.

One day in his office, Curtis shared one of the most powerful core beliefs I've now adopted.

I was trying to understand the best way to move forward with the charge of building more diversity in Wichita's entrepreneurship community through the Create Campaign and I just needed some advice from someone who found success in scaling.

Curtis listened patiently, smiling, as I ran down all of my concerns and worries. When I finished, he folded his hands, leaned forward. His smile faded. He said: "You've heard the saying, 'It's not what you know but—'"

"Who you know," I chimed in.

He shook his head sharply, adjusted his glasses and told me: "No, it's **WHO KNOWS YOU.** Never forget that."

And I didn't.

Growing a solid network is critically important to being successful. I can't stress this enough.

To make the most of a vibrant network, however, you have to possess a strong go-getter spirit. Go-getters have vision. They execute upon that vision strategically, methodically and consistently. Their sense of drive and determination is felt and demonstrated.

Pair that go-getter spirit with a strong network and watch your goals get accomplished even more rapidly. Here's why: when people know you and embrace you, they're much more inclined to make favorable decisions in regards to you. These decisions can range from making introductions and asks on your behalf to directing resources your way to help your cause.

Networking placed me on stages with multimillionaires; helped me to create a microloan fund for minority entrepreneurs and, as I've shared, allowed my nonprofit organization to be gifted an entire building in good condition to advance our work.

Networking opens access.

TO IMPACT WHO KNOWS YOU, BUILD YOUR BRAND

Your brand is your reputation. It's a promise and a message that tells people how to regard you in the professional, business and everyday spaces of work and play. Unlike corporations, which tell a more direct storyline about their capabilities, a personal brand is a bit more fluid because it incorporates personal and professional elements.

To build a dynamic personal brand, consider incorporating the following:

- The issue that drives your work
- Who you are within the work
- How the work connects with others

Once you have identified elements of your personal brand, spend time determining how you communicate about your brand.

ON SOCIAL MEDIA

If you're building a brand, no longer is social media about sharing memes, gifs or casually scrolling. Social media is a platform that helps to support – or detract – from the brand you're conveying offline.

Even on your personal social media pages, the content posted should support the brand you're building.

Your profile picture needs to be solid. No Snapchat filter profile pictures with hearts, puppy dog ears and tongues sticking out. Your cover photo area should revolve around your live, work and play time.

Posts should be frequent and original – not mere reposts of someone else's content. Your posts should also be engaging and should support the brand narrative you're building. Posts should contain a mix of words, visuals, graphics and videos. Use Facebook Live or other recording services to offer an inside view of your life and activities.

Even in this content mix, understand the balance between "you-centric" posts and posts that involve other people. No one, and I repeat no one, enjoys reading posts that are about "I, I, I." These posts are a turn off. As you determine your content ask, how does your "I" connect with the "We" and "Us" that people care about?

Comment and engage with those who react to your posts. Create opportunities for a two-way dialogue.

On company and organization pages, use your scheduling feature. Scheduling routine posts helps you use your time more effectively.

Use hashtags to further personalize content and attract followers.

My graphic design company uses #cmlcollective and #designedright when we're posting about company projects, business or accomplishments. When I'm writing about achievements in my personal life, I use the hashtag: #designingmydecade. When I'm posting about minority business development and my nonprofit, I use #letscreate (hashtags aren't punctuation-friendly, by the way).

Social media is a valuable component of creating and maintaining a compelling brand, but it's not the only medium where you need to have a viable presence. The more cohesive and consistent you are on social media, as well as through other mediums, the more successful your brand has a chance to become.

OFFLINE

With the award recognitions and, through my professional network, I received a breakthrough invitation. In 2017, my friend, Jacob Wayman, who worked with me on the Entrepreneurship Task Force, was starting a new effort through Google for Entrepreneurs called Startup Grind. Through Startup Grind, top-level CEOs were to be interviewed in a fireside-chat-style event.

Jacob invited me to be the lead interviewer.

I was hesitant, of course, wondering why he asked me out of everyone in his network.

Jacob shared that my previous skills as a reporter were needed and I was a "fresh" face; someone who wasn't always tapped for opportunities.

He didn't have to say anymore. I was in.

Our first interview was with Jeff Turner, a successful CEO of one of the nation's top aerospace parts manufacturing companies – Spirit AeroSystems. The great thing about Jeff being up first is that I had an opportunity to work with him in 2016 when the Wichita Regional Chamber of Commerce invited me to share a stage with Turner, another business leader, Scott Schwindaman and an internationally-known entrepreneur who appeared at the Chamber's annual end-of-the-year meeting.

Having the annual meeting as a point of commonality with Jeff calmed my nerves. At Startup Grind, I went into mini-Oprah mode. I confidently helped him to navigate telling his thrilling back-story of taking a declining division of a large company, turning it into an independent company and watching it thrive as a major supplier in the aerospace industry. The interview was recorded in front of a sold-out audience.

That year, I conducted each of the Startup Grind interviews, which were held monthly, at that time. I interviewed CEOs from Turner to the co-founder of Freddy's Frozen Custard & Steakburgers to even Curtis Whitten, that smooth brother I previously mentioned.

After each Startup Grind interview, I'd capture a selfie with the CEO and post it on social media. These were social-media friendly encounters and my network swelled with all of the activity.

With the increased attention, here are a few lessons that I gained:

TO BUILD YOUR BRAND GET A GOOD HEADSHOT & WRITE A STRONG BIO

You'll be asked for a bio and headshot often if you make appearances, facilitate panels or even if you attend professional events. Consider writing a longer bio for written programs and a shorter bio when you're going to have a spoken introduction.

Need help writing a good bio? Here's my template:

(Your first and last name) is a/n (insert an overview statement here... kind of like an elevator pitch about you). (Last name)'s, (insert your hometown), currently serves as (insert your current job title/position). Prior to joining the organization, (Last name) (insert a previous position) where (list an accomplishment).

(Insert a transition sentence to move bio from your professional accomplishments to your community service... i.e. Ever-involved in the community), (insert position and organization names that you're involved with). (Last name's) leadership skills have earned honors including: (list two or three awards here and the organizations they're from). (Last name), who graduated... *insert educational details here*, is (insert any family details you wish to include or a quote you live by).

Still stuck? Ask your mentors to share their resumes and bios with you for added inspiration. I got this tip after a beloved corporate executive, Terri Rice, shared hers with me.

TO BUILD YOUR BRAND CREATE A LOOK CONSISTENT WITH YOUR BRAND

As a reporter, we were told to dress for the story we were covering. In the business world, you've got to dress in a look consistent with your brand. Define your own sense of "corporate" style. I didn't even truly understand the significance of this point until late in my 30s. I was always a jeans and T-shirt kind of girl who was told through life by a variety of people that I needed to improve how I dressed and presented myself. I never had time for nail appointments or hair appointments. There was just too much work to do and, quite frankly, I never wanted to throw money at, what I previously considered, superficial purchases.

Being in the limelight, however, requires you to look the part even on a tight budget. For each Startup Grind, for example, I made sure to wear something new, which spaced out my wardrobe purchases each month — a rate my budget could tolerate.

Unsure what your style is?

It took me awhile to find mine. I used to love watching the old TLC show, *What Not to Wear*. I also was a big fan of InStyle magazines. I also talked to women whose fashion I loved. Some of the best advice came from my fashionable mother-in-law, Greta Long. I received consultations from local stylists such as Keyocsha Brown. I'd ask these ladies their approach to shopping and setting their style. I then keyed in on what type of style I liked and began selecting my apparel purchases along these lines:

> **Color** — Black is my favorite color so I began buying a lot of staple pieces that could easily be paired with a statement jewelry piece or a pattern. Leopard print is my favorite pattern. I stayed away from trendy clothing and people began complimenting me on my style.
>
> **Essentials** — Knowing I prefer pants to skirts because I get cold easily, I began buying basic pieces that could be paired across multiple outfits and that could also keep me warm. Because I also moved lots of materials in the course of a given week for my clients – from large boxes of custom-printed T-shirts to banners and more – my shoe-game had to be practical. I began trading out my heels for cute flats.
>
> I also began carrying larger tote bags that could hold my notebooks and journals. These bags ensured were practical as well as stylish. Sometimes I even carried small clutches inside of larger bags so I

could grab and go rather than carry an oversized bag to a function that required a clutch.

A rule of thumb is to dress up for those occasions when you're in front of groups. For these appearances, I always have a collection of suit jackets, jumpsuits and special dresses that I wear. I also tend to wear more make-up than usual since heavier make-up applications show better in photographs. This, again, helps to carry the brand look across multiple platforms—websites, social media, etc.

Make-up – Other than presentations, I also have go-to make-up artists: Flawless Faces by Camille owned by Camille Scott and Smash Glam's Aisha Bullocks, for special occasions. I don't wear full face all of the time but, when I do, my make-up artists knows my preferences and know when to add even more flair as the occasion calls.

Hair - I appreciate the natural hair movement that swept the country when I was in my mid-30s. Being able to embrace my natural curls, my faux locs and braided hairstyles in the corporate world was a welcome change from forcing myself to wear perms during my reporting days. Like many, perms ended up damaging my hair.

When I first went natural, my short haircut was sassy and fresh. As my hair grew out, I struggled with the in-between length look. As soon as I got enough length, I would bunch my hair up into a ponytail. If I felt fancy, I'd do a twist-out for some extra definition.

Then I met Ashlee' Norris, a hair stylist who owns Simply Beautiful Hair Salon. She encouraged me to try bold, new styles including shaving the sides of my hair for a cute, modern look.

With Ashlee', I discovered that, even while natural, I was hiding my hair into a ponytail to fit other people's perceptions of how it should look rather than defining my own hair styles.

Black women seem to be constantly bombarded with unnecessary constructs around our hair in the professional world. As the natural hair movement took shape, I'd read a number of news articles about students of color who were being punished for wearing locs or their curls and twists in school districts across our country. Locs were banned in some workplaces. In July 2019, California became the first state to ban racial discrimination based on hairstyles. Yes, *2019*.

Through Ashlee', I was able to finally be free of any hair-related stigmas I was carrying with me and I let my curls do their thing. I found my look and, even better, I felt good about my look regardless of whether I was in my own office or downtown Wichita boardrooms.

Additionally, Ashlee' shared my passion of encouraging minority business growth. She co-located several other stylists in her shop encouraging them to promote their own styling brands. Her shop is the home of Flawless Faces by Camille, my make-up artist and she even collaborated with a Black-owned nail technician, Nanette Plummer of Blaque Pearl Nails and Beauty Salon, to perform manicures at Ashlee's shop. This meant, during hair appointments, I could also get my nails done while in the chair. It was the perfect solution for on-the-go professionals.

I appreciate Ashlee' for being instrumental in helping me fall back in love with my hair.

I encourage anyone who is struggling with "hair shame" to put in the work of overcoming that shame. We have enough in life to worry about. How others perceive our hair should not be one of our worries any longer.

TO BUILD YOUR BRAND KEEP THESE ESSENTIALS IN MIND

Invest in your own name tag – Rather than wearing the sticker name badges provided, I have my own magnetic clip-on name tag. Even if you think you're going into rooms where people know you, never give them a moment to doubt. Having your name and title displayed on a larger, nice nametag helps to visually reinforce who you are every time you meet people and every time they see you.

Keep business cards on hand – There's no excuse to run out. Stay ahead of your supply and make sure to always have them handy. Whether people use them or not, having business cards helps you to easily make a connection that can be followed up on. Having cards also gives the impression that you're prepared and well put together.

Not a graphic designer? Find a freelancer, get inspiration from Google Images of other business cards or use platforms such as canva.com to design your cards. There's plenty of resources available to help you differentiate yourself and add to your professional and brand reputation.

Pro tip: If you use a designer, always request they return your master artwork files to you, as well as print-ready files, as part of your contract. By doing so, you can always have access to your graphics. Having this access is very important so that you won't have to wait for your graphic designer's timelines to place a reorder directly to a printer, for example.

Smile - People who smile are considered pleasant, approachable and engaging. The act of smiling also makes people feel happier, according to findings released in 2019 by researchers from the University of Tennessee at Knoxville.

As often as possible, wear a smile.

TO IMPACT WHO KNOWS YOU, ENHANCE YOUR BRAND

Once you've developed your brand, enhancing your brand really boils down to how you treat people. In your personal, business and private dealings, do people feel respected and appreciated in their interactions with you?

Here are a few tips:

TO ENHANCE YOUR BRAND – WRITE THANK YOU NOTES

Do you write thank you notes and mail them to people who have spent their time with you? My friend, Jacob who invited me to host Startup Grind, frequently writes notes on personalized stationary and sends a small affirmation with those notes either as a magnet, coaster or postcard.

I began to adopt that practice after receiving multiple notes from Jacob.

TO ENHANCE YOUR BRAND – BE AUTHENTIC

Another way to enhance your brand is by speaking cordially to people. I always try to be warm, inviting and authentic in my encounters with people I know and those who I do not. My authenticity with people helps to affirm my brand based on my consistency.

TO ENHANCE YOUR BRAND
BE DEPENDABLE

Another way I work to enhance my brand is to take ownership if and when I do experience a failure— no matter who is at fault.

With CML Collective, I'm ultimately the leader and the decision maker. Accepting responsibility doesn't make me a scapegoat. Quite the opposite: accepting responsibility for mistakes helps to enhance the sense of trust and transparency that people have come to expect from me and my business dealings.

One of my first out-of-state clients had a large bulk T-shirt order. I went above and beyond on the artwork design for this client after learning the artwork that the client submitted to me had to be completely redone upon the request of a department within the institution. I completed the artwork by illustration —not computer graphics — which the client loved. When transitioning the order to print production, however, my print supplier was having mechanical difficulties with his machinery that delayed the order from being delivered at the date I set with the client.

Instead of blaming my supplier, I ended up having to drive the order to the institution out of town to make up time lost by the machinery malfunction. The order ultimately got there in time for the client's event but that was such a memorable lesson for me that it prompted me to create additional protocols if one supplier failed me.

At the end of the day, the client doesn't care about my supply chain issues nor should my clients experience any sense of disruption. The client cares about their order. Period.

No excuses. Always deliver.

TO ENHANCE YOUR BRAND
BRING OTHERS ALONG

When you win, who do you bring along with you?

I spoke about participating in the Wichita Regional Chamber of Commerce's annual meeting in 2016 where I shared the stage with a business mogul. I was shocked to have even been invited to participate but it was another example of a door opening so others could see themselves through me on that stage.

What was even more compelling about that night was what happened when I stepped off the stage. Scores of other African-Americans who attended the event approached me, embraced me and said they were so proud of me.

The absolute best message following that event came from Danielle Johnson, a fierce young woman whose heart is with and for the people in Wichita. She wrote on my Facebook wall, *"When you win, we all get to win with you. Thank you for laying a path that you welcome others to walk on with open arms."* – December 2, 2016, Facebook

So, again, I'll ask: when you win, who do you bring along with you?

TO IMPACT WHO KNOWS YOU, CONQUER ROOMS

Once you build your brand, have a strategy for how to conquer rooms.

Every room is a space where you belong— whether by permission or invite. You must believe this or else the room has already conquered you.

I've often found myself as one of a few Black people or Black women, if not the only, in rooms. I was very conscious about that. I spent time convincing myself, inwardly, that I belonged at tables in these instances, but it was uncomfortable at first. I remember, with the Entrepreneurship Task Force, for example, actually sharing my concern with the two men leading the ETF in hopes to gain some advice. At that point, I trusted them with the conversation.

Their response: *"We invited you to the table for a reason. Hold nothing back. We need your voice."*

Not only did they need my voice, they created an environment that protected my voice in a space where it might otherwise have largely gone unheard. They also affirmed my voice — something quite powerful in creating a welcoming and inclusive environment.

While their help was appreciated, I also found a quote by Malcolm X, one of my favorite Civil Rights leaders, to be spot on when he said: **SITTING AT THE TABLE DOESN'T MAKE YOU A DINER, UNLESS YOU EAT SOME OF WHAT'S ON THAT PLATE.**

In other words, being at the table wasn't enough. I had to use my voice at the table so I began to speak. My words were met with great respect and put into action.

I also went to the Bible. There, I found inspiration from the Lord comforting Moses, who feared speaking because he stuttered. In another instance, the Lord provided reassurance to the prophet Jeremiah who was truly struggling with confidence about the ability to use his voice.

I read in Jeremiah Chapter 1:

4Now the word of the LORD came to me saying,
  5"Before I formed you in the womb I knew you,
    And before you were born I consecrated you;
    I have appointed you a prophet to the nations."
  6Then I said, "Alas, Lord GOD!
    Behold, I do not know how to speak,
    Because I am a youth."
  7But the LORD said to me,
    "Do not say, 'I am a youth,'
    Because everywhere I send you, you shall go,
    And all that I command you, you shall speak.
  8"Do not be afraid of them,
    For I am with you to deliver you," declares the LORD.

9THEN THE LORD STRETCHED OUT HIS HAND AND TOUCHED MY MOUTH, AND THE LORD SAID TO ME,
  "BEHOLD, I HAVE PUT MY WORDS IN YOUR MOUTH.
  10"See, I have appointed you this day over the nations and over the kingdoms,
    To pluck up and to break down,
    To destroy and to overthrow,
    To build and to plant."
  11The word of the LORD came to me saying, "What do you see, Jeremiah?" And I said, "I see a rod of an almond tree." 12Then the LORD said to me, "You have seen well, **FOR I AM WATCHING OVER MY WORD TO PERFORM IT."**

A year after joining the Entrepreneurship Task Force, the group was looking to share its accomplishments and Gary Oborny invited me to record a segment about the Create Campaign on the recap video.

It was February 2016 when that video was shared at the Chamber's annual luncheon that was held at INTRUST Bank Arena and attracted an audience of more than 500 of our city's business leaders. Sitting in the audience was Fidelity Bank President, Aaron Bastian, who I did not know at the time.

But I soon would.

March 2016, I was invited to share about the Create Campaign at Wichita Insight, another Wichita Regional Chamber of Commerce event that helped corporate executives and their spouses better acclimate to the city.

I was one of several presenters at that evening's event. I concluded my presentation feeling slightly bummed that my talk didn't go over as well as I'd hoped it would. Everyone was ready to eat and it seemed my presentation was in between them doing just that. Once dinner was served, I found myself in a great conversation about parenting and dietary preferences with a delightful woman named Michelle. We talked at length that night and I remember leaving the event thinking that the conversation was nice during what, otherwise, was a lackluster occasion.

Within a few days of that presentation, I received a call. It was Aaron, who turned out to be Michelle's husband. He shared that he saw my video at the Chamber's luncheon and that it was one of the more interesting features of the program. He said he had meant to reach out to me then but that task got lost among other items on his to do list. He went on to say that his wife came home from the Wichita Insight meeting and told him he and I had to connect. He invited me to meet with him to discuss the Create Campaign.

I accepted the invitation and prepared my pitch to gain his support.

In April 2016, I met Aaron face-to-face in his executive conference room at Fidelity Bank. I was quite nervous but managed to make my way through that presentation pretty well. As I concluded, Aaron said it was nice to hear about the Create Campaign. He then extended an opportunity that I wasn't expecting: he wanted to meet with me, regularly, to learn more about my work and my story.

That began our work together.

Over a series of lunches, we explored challenges and barriers minority founders experienced in entrepreneurship. Conversations weren't always easy as we began to discuss the dynamics of race and privilege.

There was one conversation I distinctly remember at AVI Seabar and Chophouse that left me grabbing my side of the lunch table because of the differences in our perspectives. We committed to staying at the table that day to discuss and sort out difficult assumptions about race and privilege.

That was a pivotal point for both of us and it launched our efforts to create a microloan fund for founders of color in Wichita.

Fast-forward to 2018 when I was invited to speak at the Wichita Downtown Rotary Club – one of the most privileged rooms in our city. Downtown Rotary was working to grow its diversity while implementing its mission to improve the lives of others in communities at home and around the world. I had been invited to give a talk on diversity and inclusion.

Who introduced me?

Aaron Bastian.

"Good afternoon," he began. *"Today, I have the honor of introducing Christina Long. I sat amongst you all and heard a lot of introductions. Most of them include the word 'honor,' too. But I've chosen 'honor' for this introduction and I do so very purposefully. Simply put: I am in awe of Christina Long. She's an entrepreneur, a mentor to other entrepreneurs through her nonprofit, Create Campaign, a champion for minority entrepreneurship in our community. She displays an unparalleled passion for her work and she pushes me harder than anyone I've met in Wichita. I just see the look on her face. She knows it's true. Recently, Christina was named the young professional of the year by the Wichita Regional Chamber of Commerce due largely to her efforts in leading diversity and inclusion efforts not only in our community but statewide. It is our shared belief that the only way we can move forward as a city is together, all of us linked in the charge to build a better Wichita. This work is not easy, but nothing worth fighting for ever is. So, yes, I chose the word 'honor' to introduce Christina because I truly believe she is critical to our future in Wichita. Please join me in welcoming, Christina Long."*

That day, I conquered the room.

At the head table cheering me on were my husband, our friend, Kyle Ellison, who is now the Executive Director of Real Men, Real Heroes, a nonprofit organization to help mentor boys, several members of Wichita Urban Professionals and, my photographer, Danielle Gauna of Danielle Marie Photography. She helped capture the moment.

There's nothing wrong with being confident in spaces where you might otherwise feel inadequate. Your confidence is a must.

FOR THE greater SUCCESS

To conquer rooms:

- Work the room. Do not be a bystander. Be actively engaged in making your presence known and felt.

- Shake hands firmly. A weak handshake leaves much to question.

- Act interested; not overwhelmed. You belong. Carry that with you.

- Make genuine connections with those of like minds. Small talk is petty. Perform recon and get to learn about those who share the room with you.

- Be introduced and, don't hesitate to introduce yourself. As a matter of position, many people wait to be introduced by others. Don't hesitate. Introduce yourself. Be humble and approachable in that way.

- Don't answer all the questions; speak on the important ones with clarity, precision and conviction. In the school district, we called it "hogs and logs." Don't hog conversations by dominating them and don't be forgettable by not participating. Interject mindfully and artfully in conversations.

- Never sit in the back of the room. Sit close to the presenter or in a visible place at the front of the room. Enhance the room with your presence.

FOR THE greater SUCCESS

- Be as punctual as possible – 10 minutes early is the sweet-spot. Five minutes early is on time. On time is late. Don't be late.

- Once you've established yourself as a presence in the room, it's imperative, particularly as people of color, to bring others into the room. Who else can you invite into rooms you were once invited into?

I'll say it like the PBS special, *Boss: The Black Experience in Business* stated: **"ONCE YOU GET IN, YOU DON'T JUST LOOK OUT FOR SELF. YOU LOOK OUT FOR THOSE WHO ARE COMING BEHIND YOU. THAT IS THE PRICE OF LEADERSHIP AND THE PRICE OF WANTING TO MAKE A DIFFERENCE."**

TO IMPACT WHO KNOWS YOU, FOLLOW UP

Networking is only as good as your ability to follow up.

Hand-in-hand with the work are conversations over lunch and coffee. Use meal times as networking extension and enhancement times. Budget your time and resources appropriately to make the best use of this practice.

For those who you wish to get to know, have a clear agenda for the encounter otherwise your conversation may be fraught with small talk in the grand scheme of things.

For those who are game-changers in your viewpoint, schedule regular meetings and vigorously protect that time.

During these conversations, move through your conversation and agenda but also be mindful enough to take note about people's likes, dislikes and their mannerisms. Remember important happenings and important people in your contact's lives so that, when you see them again, you can sprinkle those names and happenings in the conversation. Being personal— and personable— helps you be memorable and encourages those who follow up with you to continue making time to do so because it's time well-spent.

I already shared how networking created a wonderful connection for me in Aaron Bastian. There are plenty of others who have gained a better sense of who I am in this work over coffees and conversations.

Take the time to make and nurture these connections so that, when you leave these tables and go back into the world, you have people who will fight for you and with you because they have a strong belief in you.

It's an incredible feeling to be thought of.

Being thought of happens when people know you.

Who knows you?

Control the ground the land

"YOU HAVE TO CONTROL THE LAND. YOU CAN HAVE ALL THE VISIONS BUT, UNTIL YOU CONTROL THAT GROUND AND IT'S YOURS, YOU'RE AT THE MERCY OF OTHER PEOPLE. AND OTHER PEOPLE HAVE OTHER AGENDAS,"

- Chris Lee, entrepreneur and mentor

In all of this work, there's a growing common denominator that infrequently gets discussed in leadership conversations and that's the conversation around our earnings and how we deploy our income for community uplift.

In the years I'd been managing my nonprofit work while balancing my for-profit client load, I was not reaching my full earnings potential. I created my business to provide professional design services to communities of color so that our efforts, companies and initiatives could also have a compelling visual presence. I learned early on that a professional presence helps create a more positive perception of capabilities and aptitude and I wanted to make sure these firms had the look just like any other firm would have.

In doing so, I entered a volume-play business model. My pricing was well below market on the for-profit side which meant I had to work a higher volume of jobs in order to make a profit. That play lasted six years. Along the way, I gained some larger organization and corporate clients who were thrilled at my pricing even as I began inching it closer to market rate, particularly with all of the experience I gained and the value that came to my client endeavors because their professional presence was solidly intact.

When taking a look at my pricing, my mentor, Dell Gines, whom I've referenced a few times already, came through with, yet, a whole new set of lessons in year five and six of my company.

Dell shared: **"TIME IS DIRECTLY CONNECTED TO REVENUE. WHAT YOU NEED TO CONSIDER IS HOW TO TRADE TIME FOR DOLLARS AT SCALE."**

He shared, **"DON'T START WITH 'WHAT IS YOUR BUDGET?' KNOW YOUR VALUE,"** he said. **"BUDGETS CAN BE ADJUSTED."**

Boom.

Game changed. As I was working to reclaim my time, a larger shift needed to occur and represents my company's current restructuring plan. All of this to say, we can work as hard as we want to providing value and uplift for community advancement but, if we're not financially strong, we're not as effective as we can be. It's true that money isn't the solution for all situations but money is a tool that can be leveraged to help influence change.

"Christina, when you look at your community, the Black community, you have a lot of good, well-meaning leaders but, if you look at your political leaders, they're nice people but they can't rub two nickels together," one leader shared with me.

Ouch.

It's no secret that there is a racial wealth gap. When looking specifically at Black wealth, one needs to understand the role that slavery, Jim Crow, separate but equal and bias in housing and lending policies played in creating the gap. As the *Washington Post* recently wrote, "when one system of economic oppression collapsed, new ones were created to fill the void."

According to the article, "the typical black family has about 1/10th of the wealth of a typical white family," (See: "Why the racial wealth gap persists, more than 150 years after emancipation" June 19, 2019)

Wealth inequity, being underinvested in and having disproportionate business ownership rates have impacted the rate of economic growth within Wichita's Black community.

HASHTAGS DON'T BUY BLOCKS

When we begin to have a stronger financial foundation, we're able to gain access to tables and conversations we'd otherwise not be privy to. We begin to be among the power players who have the brand – and the clout—to accelerate movements that are too often resource-depleted.

Even in my own experience, the Create Campaign's ability to attract financial resources helped our organization to move more swiftly through our programming build-out. It also set us up to be in a more sound financial position to accept the building that was gifted to us. Had we been financially vulnerable, that gift would have been contributed elsewhere or the desire to gift the building could have transitioned to a traditional real estate venture. I also give credit to having a great relationship with Create Campaign's attorney, Richard Stevens. By trusting him to help negotiate contractual terms on our behalf, we were able to confidently assume ownership of the building.

Because we were in a position to first, be thought of because of our impact and branding, then to be financially solvent enough to take on the building, we now have more than a symbol of advancing inclusive entrepreneurship in our city. We have a physical, tangible, brick and mortar location in the heart of an underinvested in to create a hub that will directly benefit the economics of the area.

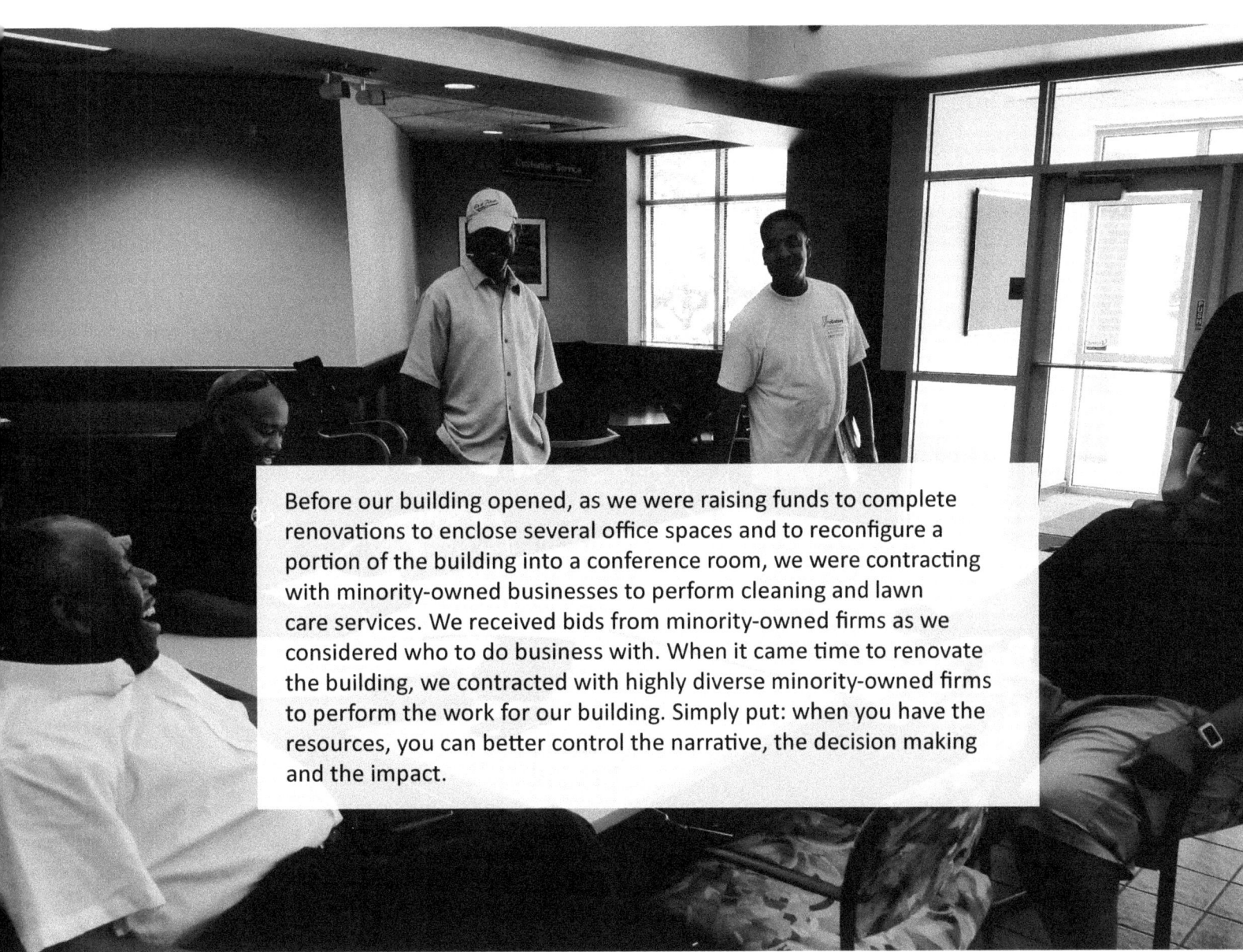

Before our building opened, as we were raising funds to complete renovations to enclose several office spaces and to reconfigure a portion of the building into a conference room, we were contracting with minority-owned businesses to perform cleaning and lawn care services. We received bids from minority-owned firms as we considered who to do business with. When it came time to renovate the building, we contracted with highly diverse minority-owned firms to perform the work for our building. Simply put: when you have the resources, you can better control the narrative, the decision making and the impact.

The value of ownership magnifies the ability to have control and can help spur change more rapidly.

Currently, there's an entire movement of celebrities and others "buying the block" as a direct action against the practice of gentrification or buying and developing properties in poorer neighborhoods in ways that displace current residents. As endearing as buying the block is, it's also not the reality for so many communities of color in our nation. As a people, too few of us have the earnings potential to buy the block. Community Reinvestment Act dollars — or funds that financial institutions are to use to help uplift low to moderate income communities — some grant funds, foundation funds and some corporate community engagement dollars may provide some assistance in this area. To truly buy the block, though, we need people willing to take bold action and position resources to make sure that our blocks are bought with integrity followed by longevity plans to care for these blocks after they're bought.

I've been invited into venture capital rooms where entrepreneurs pitch their companies to potential investors. The air in these rooms seems different than the air that I breathe, at times. Of course, there is little to no racial or ethnic diversity in these rooms; limited gender diversity, as well. And these rooms exist everywhere.

I'm looking forward to helping make these rooms more accessible. As Aaron Bastian says, even in these rooms, **"THE ISSUES ARE THE SAME. THE ZEROES ARE DIFFERENT."**

There is great potential to initiate hope and prosperity in underinvested in communities. However, we have to see value within these areas, ourselves.

I was asked, flat-out by one potential investor why Create Campaign, Inc. would spend one hundred-plus thousand dollars to renovate the building that was gifted to us? Why wouldn't we just sell the building and operate upon the proceeds from the sale?

I was shocked the question was asked so directly and, more so, that the opportunity for impact wasn't, in itself, enough to articulate the need for investment.

On the flip side, there is something to be said about the perceived void of visible investors of color in our city. Whether they deploy their funds outside of Wichita or deploy them to certain projects quietly, their perceived lack of formal giving activity is daunting. I know those who are giving significant, investment-level dollars are overly-stretched but, imagine, what could be accomplished if a more collective, strategic and *public* sense of investment and funds deployment occurred within communities of color.

Trust, I understand the income inequality overly impacting our communities but I also know that we have a number of dynamic, successful breakouts who have the financial wherewithal to diversify these investor rooms. I'm concerned. And, whether they've been invited in or not, it says something that *I'm* being asked who to invite.

While I'm not an accountant or a financial manager, there are some things others have shared with me that I've found helpful to begin my own journey to credit repair and wealth accumulation:

TO CONTROL THE GROUND; CONTROL THE LAND, MAKE TIME TO ORGANIZE HOW YOU CAPTURE INFORMATION ABOUT YOUR FINANCES

More than being familiar with the ins and outs of your income and expenses, set some revenue goals if you own a business or income goals and watch the trends of how your money is moving. Use the details to make decisions about your household budget or your company's operations.

I mentioned having a volume play when I first got into business. That business model did not meet my profit goals. It was also a time drainer.

That saying "time is money" is cliché, but so true.

In-person meetings with potential clients began to drain my time and budget. Consider a simple client inquiry: "I have a marketing concept and I'd like to meet with you about it." While I appreciate opportunities to meet with potentially new clients, how I went about it wasn't very efficient. Initially, I'd schedule the meeting at a neutral location such as a coffee shop and, not only have the cost of mileage and time away from working on existing client work, but I'd also have the time of conversing with the potential client. If the potential client didn't contract with me, then nothing netted from these meet ups except mileage and meal expenses on my books.

Once I looked at the monetary drain from this practice I decided to cease the practice of client intake coffees. I created questionnaires for the pre-client to complete then scheduled a phone call about the process with them. In-person meetings were reserved for existing clients with very few exceptions.

This practice, though less personal, helped me to deliver better services to clients who decided to contract with my company while also making better use of my resources.

TO CONTROL THE GROUND; CONTROL THE LAND,
PAY ATTENTION

Beyond your business books, just paying closer attention to our personal financial goals is a must for our financial health and fitness.

- Keep close watch on our credit scores. Credit trackers such as Capital One's CreditWise or Credit Karma may be helpful for you.

- Pay bills on time. Don't let bills go into slow pay status or, worse, collections.

- Curtail impulsive buys and look at ways to stretch our coins… all of these things matter when it comes to developing a financial savviness that will have you operating with well more than "two nickels."

- Create a financial dashboard that contains at-a-glance indicators of your company or organization's financial fitness.

    I found these books to be helpful: *The Essentials of Finance and Accounting for Non-Financial Managers* by Edward Fields and *Managing by the Numbers: A Commonsense Guide to Understanding and Using Your Company's Financials* by Chuck Kremer

TO CONTROL THE GROUND; CONTROL THE LAND,
NEGOTIATE

I never learned how to negotiate. My first job offer, I accepted the rate flat-out. Little did I know, it would set me up to play from behind my entire career as a reporter. I'd never earn what my value was. Beyond corporate America, the same happened as an entrepreneur bidding one of my first contract jobs. I had no idea that just making a little more than what I was making in the workplace was not the move.

Of course, the client accepted my overly-low bid. It was a steal for them. Being self-employed, my rate didn't take into account estimated quarterly taxes, market rate for others providing the same service in my industry, etc. I lost that first year so much so that, when it was time for contract renegotiations, I was nervous to share that the client would be getting fewer hours than the previous contract because of adjustments. The client understood and accepted the terms because they knew what happened. And allowed it.

We have to learn how to defend ourselves and proper negotiations training is part of building a strong defense.

Too often, one of the attorneys I know, Sam Foreman would say, regarding negotiations, **"YOU DON'T WANT TO LEAVE ANYTHING ON THE TABLE THAT IT WOULD TAKE TO ACCOMPLISH YOUR MISSION."**

Determine what you need and ask for it.

FOR THE greater SUCCESS

One of my dear friends, Gaye Tibbets, is a highly-accomplished attorney. She presented a training that spoke about negotiating during a women's leadership conference I helped to create.

Her tips for learning to negotiate for what you are worth:

- Read the book, *Ask For It: How Women Can Use the Power of Negotiation to Get What They Really Want* by Linda Babcock
- Practice – either with a friend or in front of a mirror, practice so it becomes natural when you negotiate for real
- Articulate your value – document the rationale that creates a basis for negotiating
- Do your homework and know your market salary if negotiating a salary change

Her source: https://www.pon.harvard.edu/daily/salary-negotiations/negotiate-salary-3-winning-strategies/

You may also find some great negotiations resources by visiting: https://www.appointmentsproject.org/

TO CONTROL THE GROUND; CONTROL THE LAND, THE SEASON OF WORK

There are times in your life where you'll be in a season of quiet, lonely work. It's a season of preparation.

In his book, *Rules of the Red Rubber Ball*, author Kevin Carroll describes this season like this:

"PREPARATION MEANS DOING WORK THAT IS CALLED THE LONELY WORK: THE UNGLAMOROUS TASKS THAT NO ONE TELLS YOU TO DO AND THE HARD WORK THAT NO ONE WILL NOTICE."

It's the grind that people don't always want to talk about because, true to its name, the grind is hard.

As a business owner, I've had 24-hour shifts. I've had bouts of depression feeling overwhelmed, overworked, undervalued and like I was losing my natural mind.

In this season, it's not fun.

It's about focus and grit.

You have to will your wins during this season.

It's, as my attorney friend Sam Foreman calls it, **"THE PAIN OF GROWING."**

It's the place where Aaron Bastian says, **"YOU REALIZE THE RESPONSIBILITY OF WHAT YOU CREATED."**

And you cannot walk away.

It's in this space where processes get refined.

Case in point:

Because I value networking, I valued being accessible and available. And, while I was growing my brand, I needed to be as accessible as possible.

Then, the shift happened.

I was starting to be inundated by all kinds of requests: requests to help people start their business, answer questions about their ideas, of course clients wanting to meet from my graphic design firm, strategic consulting requests from well-esteemed companies and organizations interested in reaching more authentically into communities of color… the list went on and on.

I struggled to manage it all.

I wore my Google calendar out. I tried an automatic scheduler app, Acuity, based on my preloaded availability. That worked for awhile but, what that didn't do, was filter meetings. To filter meetings, I still had to speak with someone to schedule meetings and that, combined with everything else I needed to accomplish during my workdays and nights, and I couldn't reach everyone. It was a growing aggravation.

I began to drop balls all over the place – the absolute worst play for a perfectionist.

I tried bringing in other help – a fabulous intern and some creative contractors since I was unable to hire part-time or full-time workers. That provided a whole series of leadership lessons that I'm still learning.

Needless to say, I was miserable.

FOR THE *greater* SUCCESS

In times of overwhelm, you must look at your processes.

- Are you protecting your time?
- Are you setting boundaries?
- Are you taking care of yourself? As my friend, Marquetta Atkins, asks: "How's your spirit?"
- Are you running your days or are your days running you?

Here are some tips I was able to gain out of my misery:

- Limit accessibility – Assess whether meetings you call are truly warranted. Those that are, determine if in-person, phone calls or video conferencing are viable options.

- Stack meetings – Assign one day as meeting day and stack meetings. Create a max on the number of meetings you'll have in one day and in one week.

- Protect your limits – Once you've reached meeting limits for a given day or week, schedule for the next day or week. Push out meetings. The work will either happen electronically or it can wait. It's OK if some work waits as long as you have the ethic to make sure not to miss important deadlines or deliverables. Rarely do I miss deadlines.

FOR THE greater SUCCESS

- Check emails at given times of day rather than throughout the day, if possible – Email can be a time-sucker. Close social media apps and email apps and dedicate work time to work time.

- Prioritize tasks – Every task cannot hold your most important, top slot. If this is the case, nothing can get done well. Prioritize tasks and work accordingly.

- Carve out a self-care routine and protect that time – Caring for yourself is one of the most important things you can do in life. Self-care is nurturing yourself. It doesn't mean always hopping on flights to clear your mind. Finding clarity daily is true self care.

- Reconnect with friends – The laughs with Ashlee', the inside jokes between my girl, Jordan, the lunch interventions with my friends, Ami, Jaya, Richard, Ted, and more, proved to be tremendously helpful and quite necessary.

- Avoid distractions and breathe.

- Recite self-affirmations.

- Eat. Consistently. Never be too busy to fuel your body with the proper nutrients.

FOR THE greater SUCCESS

- Sleep.
- Laugh.
- Listen to music.
- Unplug. Set boundaries for your own screen time. Too many bosses have made their beds extensions of their offices. You, ma'am, you sir, put the work away, fix that pillow and rest.
- In the words of Auntie Maxine (Representative Maxine Waters), **"RECLAIM YOUR TIME."**

When you have found a proper balance of self and work, you can more easily bring your best, most rested and refreshed self to work to make greater impact.

If you decide not to take care of yourself, trust me, life has a way of forcing you to.

At some point, we all reach capacity. I've been living here. There are going to be some major changes and I hope that everyone who is affected will be understanding.

Sometimes you have to let go to fly! #designingmydecade

Part 1 of the transition: we're maxed on clients, projects and bookings. Please see below for referrals.

Part 2: limited engagements/ limited contact
While I love to support as much as I can, I am taking a break from speaking and presenting unless already on the books.
During this time - email is the best way to connect.
Limited in-person meetings are reserved for existing clients, collaborators and friends. Please do not take offense.

Part 3: support
I could use some more. If you know an entrepreneur who can benefit from the Create Campaign, please connect them to the resources, our page, events & our website.
For me - Say a prayer. Send an encouraging thought. If you see me out, please don't ask me if I'm tired. I am.
This, too, is part of the journey. It's part of the sacrifice to try to make a change. It's part of work/life balance, seasons and rhythms. It's the life I have chosen to live and the life I must now better manage. Much love.

- Facebook entries June 11, 2019

Here are a few books that helped me adopt better self-care:

- *In the Meantime* audio book– Iyanla Vanzant
- *Yesterday, I Cried* – Iyanla Vanzant
- *Rules of the Red Rubber Ball* – Kevin Carroll
- *The 7 Habits of Highly Effective People* – Stephen Covey

Conclusion

There's no natural conclusion to self-growth and evolution.

But there is one final thought I wish to share: as you find your way through the seasons of work, life and play, what is critically important is remaining true to who you are in each and every space.

My husband, Jonathan, puts it this way: **"AUTHENTICITY IS THE GOLDEN STANDARD OF LEADERSHIP."**

So, as you navigate, take up space. Let the world know you are here. You are present. You are necessary and you matter.

Find your center.

Find your peace.

Find your strength.

Find your battle.

And be brilliant within it.

Understand the life of the worker, the influencer and the game changer is a full life because you're working in a space of time, opportunity and impact. When those three align, the results are magnified across moments and, if you really get it right...

ACROSS GENERATIONS.

PHOTOGRAPH CREDITS

All photographs used with permission.

Front Cover and Back Cover photo: Tiffany N. Cody

P. 4,5 - The Wichita Regional Chamber of Commerce

P. 6, 7, 10, 11, 18, 21, 30, 31, 35, 55, 72, 81, 82, 89, 90, 99- Christina M. Long

P. 12 - Tiffany N. Cody

P. 16 - Woods Family Archive

P. 25 - Fernando Salazar, Fernando Salazar Photography

P. 26 - Ricky Lasley, TeenView Magazine

P. 28 - Danielle Gauna, Danielle Marie Photography

P. 29 - Wichita Urban Professionals, Christina M. Long, Editor; Magazine Cover Photo Credit: Christina M. Long

P. 36 - Malcolm U. Gilmore-Long

P. 39 - Danielle Gauna, Danielle Marie Photography

P. 52 - Courtesy photo used with permission from Dell Gines

P. 60 - Christina M. Long photos taken with permission of those featured

P. 61 - Michael E. Woods, Photography by Michael E. Woods, LLC; Tiffany N. Cody, Tiffany N. Cody, J. Cousin Photography

P. 63 - Ashlee' Norris, Simply Beautiful Hair Salon; Make-up by Flawless Faces by Camille

P. 64 - Ashlee' Norris

P. 73, 74 - Danielle Gauna, Danielle Marie Photography

P. 97, 103 - Tiffany N. Cody

THANK YOU

CONTACT
CHRISTINA M. LONG:

www.cmlcollective.com

@cmlcollective

**For speaking engagements,
please email:
booking@cmlcollective.com**